Wild Orchids

OF THE MIDDLE ATLANTIC STATES

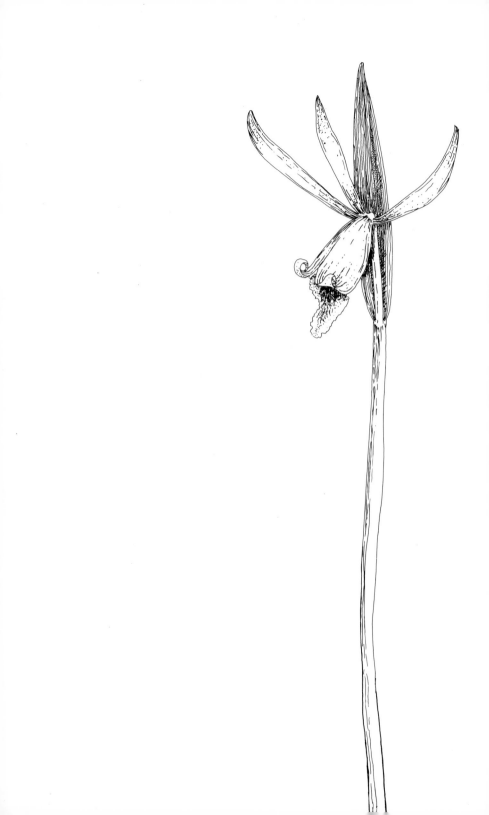

Wild Orchids

OF THE MIDDLE ATLANTIC STATES

Oscar W. Gupton and Fred C. Swope

KNOXVILLE: THE UNIVERSITY OF TENNESSEE PRESS

ACKNOWLEDGMENTS:

A substantial saving in time spent and in distance traveled resulted from assistance graciously given in locating some of the species. In appreciation of this sincere thanks are proffered to Joe Pinson, Richard D. Porcher, Jr., Gerald Roe, Robert C. Simpson, Charles C. Stevens, and Donna M.E. Ware.

Library of Congress Cataloging in Publication Data

Gupton, Oscar, W.
    Wild orchids of the Middle Atlantic States.

    Bibliography: p.
    Includes index.
    1. Orchids—Middle Atlantic States—Identification. 2. Botany—Middle Atlantic States. I. Swope, Fred C. II. Title.
QK495.O64G84   1987   584′.15′0975   86-4349
ISBN 0-87049-509-7 (alk. paper)

To Oscar W. Gupton, Sr.
and J.R. Brunner

Contents

Usual floral arrangement

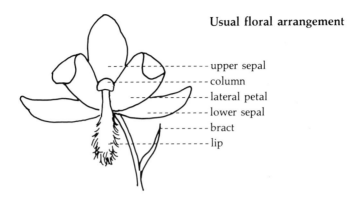

- - - - - upper sepal
- - - - - column
- - - - - lateral petal
- - - - - lower sepal
- - - - - bract
- - - - - lip

"Upside down" flower

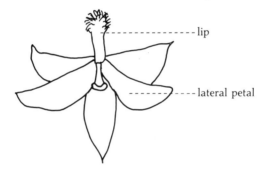

- - - - - - lip

- - - - - - lateral petal

Flower with spur

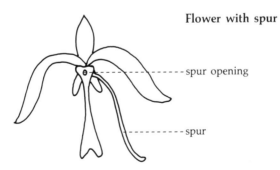

- - - - - - spur opening

- - - - - - spur

Introduction

The varicolored mantle of plants that softens the hard lines of the earth provides a source of ornamental material that is used to beautify home and workplace, and hardly any commemorative occasion is without floral decorations. Many kinds of plants are highly regarded for one or another of their attractive features, but the orchids have long held a premier position with respect to the combinations of superb colors and fanciful shapes exhibited by their flowers.

The mention of orchids usually brings to mind those species from the tropical parts of the world that are normally purchased from the florist. There are striking orchids, however, that are native to the central portion of the eastern United States and more species of them than most people realize. In some orchids the spectacular size and color found in the commercial forms are not evident; nevertheless even in the smallest flower among them a close look will reveal the interesting characteristic structure of the orchid family, and most of the time some intricate and attractive patterns of pigmentation.

Almost every one of these orchids is rare to begin with, and many of the kinds of places where orchids grow best have been and are still being decimated by gross disturbance of the land. In particular the draining of low woods, bogs, and swamps, followed by the erection of buildings and paving of roads upon these sites, has steadily reduced the number of top quality orchid habitats. If there is more general understanding of the problem and more awareness of the kind of natural beauty that is slipping away, perhaps a greater effort will be made to prevent further loss.

There are those who believe that information pertaining

to rare species should not be made public, that this information serves as a guide for those who would destroy. The belief here is that knowledge of the rarity of these beautiful plants and realization that many human activities endanger their very survival will help to engender a spirit of protection rather than destruction.

Appreciation of the orchids that grow wild in this region would be heightened if more people were familiar with these plants — what they look like, their names, where they live, their unusual features. To that end the contents of this book are organized to enable the reader to identify the species in the easiest manner possible. Each of the included species is shown in a color photograph, and each photograph is accompanied by a descriptive text written in non-technical language that requires no background in botanical vocabulary. All photographic work was done in the field under natural light conditions.

There are fifty-two species depicted that are members of twenty genera. With the exception of Florida all genera occurring in the eastern United States are represented. The species of West Virginia, Maryland, Delaware, Kentucky, Virginia, Tennessee, North Carolina, and South Carolina are treated. Seven species were not photographed, but each one is cited in the text along with its identifying characters, and it is entered as a part of the text of the species that it most resembles.

Many of these species are present in much of the surrounding territory, as indicated by the ranges given in each of the texts, so the manual is useful far beyond the borders of x the eight cited states.

It is characteristic of many species of the orchid family to "disappear." After a normal period of flowering during a given year there may be no part of the plant visible above ground the following year or in some cases for several years. The flowering cycle then will be resumed. Should a visit to a recommended site turn up nothing, it is often worthwhile to try again another year.

In the general makeup of the orchid flower there are three lower or outermost parts called sepals. Next inside or above the sepals are three petals. Sepals and petals may be similar to each other or quite dissimilar. In almost all species the lower petal or "lip" is different from the other two petals in size, shape, or color, and commonly there is a difference in all three. In a few species the flower is "turned upside down" with the lip on top. As a matter of fact the lip started out on top, and it is the majority that has turned upside down or shifted position as the young flower twisted during development.

The reproductive organs in the center of the flower of most plants are separate and distinct. In the orchids the stamens from which pollen is shed, the stigma that receives the pollen, and the style that connects the stigma to the seed-forming chamber deep within the base of the flower are fused into a "column" that varies from species to species in size, shape, and color.

The accompanying diagrams show the basic positions of the parts of the flower, an upside down flower, and a spurred flower. These parts may be almost any shape or color. Positions may vary from those shown in the diagrams. For example, in the genus *Habenaria* sepals and petals form a hood, while in *Cypripedium* the two lower sepals are fused together behind the lip.

In some species there is a tubular "spur" that originates from the base of the lip on its underside and extends backward and usually downward from the flower.

A bract or modified leaf often grows from the stem or flower stalk beneath the flower. The bract may resemble the other leaves but is usually much smaller and often scalelike.

Once again, the family Orchidaceae is not present in abundance anywhere in our range, and the records show that in many parts of the land rather large populations existed in the past that today are drastically reduced in size or are no longer with us. It is well to remember that all we will have in the future is what we save now.

Oscar W. Gupton
Fred C. Swope

Virginia Military Institute
Lexington, Virginia

Format

The species are arranged in six groups according to flower color in the following order: white, green, yellow, orange, pink, and purple. Within each of the color groups the arrangement follows the order of flowering time. The information pertaining to each species is given in the same order throughout:

Common name of the species

Scientific name of the species

Description:

General appearance of the plant as a whole or of some part having a special quality is mentioned.

Size is stated by a comment on the overall height of the plant.

Leaf character is indicated with respect to shape, size, arrangement, or position.

Flower color variations known to occur are noted.

Flowering period is given. Specific time of flowering will usually vary with the location of the plant in the region.

Other similar species that might cause misidentification are cited along with their distinguishing characters.

Varieties common to the area have their distinguishing characters described.

Miscellaneous general interest items may be included.

Other common names used for the species are given.

Habitat or type of natural environment in which the plant grows is indicated.

Range of the species in the United States is given in a pattern beginning in the northeast, then extending south, and finally west.

The scientific names in general follow the eighth edition of Gray's *Manual of Botany* and the *Manual of the Vascular Flora of the Carolinas.*

As a guide to the pronunciation of scientific names, the symbols ` and ´ are included. They mark the syllable to be accented, and the former calls for a long vowel sound, while the latter calls for a short vowel sound.

USING COLOR IN IDENTIFICATION

There are endless combinations of delicate gradations and subtle shadings in plant colors, and everyone does not see, focus upon, or describe colors exactly alike. Despite these differences in perception the use of color is a relatively simple way to begin identification.

The color groups are based primarily on petal color, and orchid flowers frequently have sepals the same color as petals. When there are two or more colors the dominant one is used for placement of the species in a color group. In these instances colors of plant parts other than the flower may be used. Should the color of a plant appear to fit in one of the color groups yet not match up with the other features, then another color group should be tried.

Some common trouble spots are:

A plant with two or more colors may usually show one color more strikingly than the others but sometimes may vary so that one of the other colors is more conspicuous. This often happens with small white, green, or yellow flowers.

Very pale yellow or green flowers may be difficult to distinguish from white.

Yellow and green frequently blend with one very slightly stronger than the other.

Orange and yellow sometimes blend into one another, and some species show variations from one to the other.

Pink and purple often blend, and deep pink is often seen as red.

The works listed below are plant manuals with keys for identification consisting of detailed technical characters:

Fernald, M.L. 1950. *Gray's Manual of Botany*. Eighth edition. New York: American Book Company.
Gleason, M.A. 1952. *Illustrated Flora of the Northeastern United States and Adjacent Canada*. The New York Botanical Garden.

Luer, C.A. 1975. *The Native Orchids of the United States and Canada excluding Florida.* The New York Botanical Garden.
Radford, A.E., H.E. Ahles, and C.R. Bell. 1968. *Manual of the Vascular Flora of the Carolinas.* Chapel Hill: University of North Carolina Press.

Species Included in Each Color Group

White

Calopogon pallidus Pale Grass Pink
Cleistes divaricata Rosebud Orchid
Goodyera pubescens Downy Rattlesnake Plantain
Goodyera repens var. *ophioides* Lesser Rattlesnake Plantain
Habenaria blephariglottis White Fringed Orchid
Habenaria nivea Snowy Orchid
Habenaria orbiculata Round-leaved Orchid
Spiranthes cernua Nodding Ladies' Tresses
Spiranthes gracilis Slender Ladies' Tresses
Spiranthes grayi Little Ladies' Tresses
Spiranthes lucida Shining Ladies' Tresses
Spiranthes praecox Grass-leaved Ladies' Tresses
Spiranthes vernalis Spring Ladies' Tresses
Triphora trianthophora Three Birds

Green

Epidendrum conopseum Green-fly Orchid
Epipactis helleborine Broad-leaved Helleborine
Habenaria viridis var. *bracteata* Long-bracted Orchid
Isotria medeoloides Small Whorled Pogonia
Isotria verticillata Large Whorled Pogonia
Liparis loeselii Yellow Twayblade
Listera smallii Appalachian Twayblade

Malaxis spicata Florida Adder's Mouth
Malaxis unifolia Green Adder's Mouth
Ponthieva racemosa Shadow Witch

Yellow

Corallorhiza trifida Pale Coral Root
Cypripedium calceolus Yellow Lady's Slipper
Habenaria clavellata Little Club-spur Orchid
Habenaria flava var. *herbiola* Southern Rein Orchid
Habenaria lacera Ragged Fringed Orchid
Habenaria repens Water Spider Orchid

Orange

Habenaria x *bicolor* Bicolored Fringed Orchid
Habenaria ciliaris Yellow Fringed Orchid
Habenaria cristata Crested Fringed Orchid
Habenaria integra Yellow Fringeless Orchid

Pink

Arethusa bulbosa Dragon's Mouth
Calopogon barbatus Bearded Grass Pink
Calopogon pulchellus Grass Pink
Cypripedium acaule Pink Lady's Slipper

Cypripedium reginae Queen Lady's Slipper
Orchis spectabilis Showy Orchid
Pogonia ophioglossoides Rose Pogonia

Purple

Aplectrum hyemale Putty Root
Corallorhiza maculata Spotted Coral Root
Corallorhiza odontorhiza Autumn Coral Root
Corallorhiza wisteriana Spring Coral Root
Eulophia ecristata Spiked Medusa
Habenaria peramoena Purple Fringeless Orchid
Habenaria psychodes Purple Fringed Orchid
Hexalectris spicata Crested Coral Root
Liparis lilifolia Large Twayblade
Listera australis Southern Twayblade
Tipularia discolor Cranefly Orchid

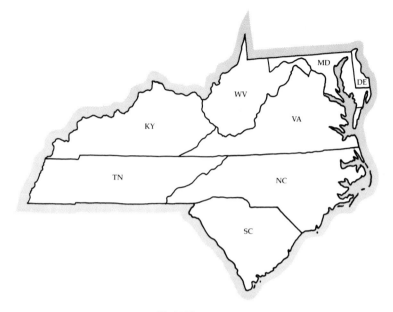

The Middle Atlantic States

Wild Orchids

OF THE MIDDLE ATLANTIC STATES

Spring Ladies' Tresses

Spiránthes vernàlis

The earliest of the ladies' tresses to flower, Spring Ladies' Tresses is also the tallest, frequently approaching four
feet (1.2m) in height. There are three to five grasslike leaves
two inches to one foot (.5–3dm) long at or near the base of
the stem. Finely and densely hairy flower clusters two to ten
inches (.5–2.5dm) long develop from March to July. White to
yellowish flowers are one quarter to one half inch (6.2–12.5mm)
long with the lip curved down and under. They are arranged
in a single spiral or occasionally along one side of the stalk.
S. laciniata, Lace-lip Ladies' Tresses, has fewer and knobbed
hairs, while *S. longilabris,* Long-lip Ladies' Tresses, has flared,
long-lipped flowers usually ordered in a straight line. Spring
Ladies' Tresses is also called Narrow-leaved Ladies' Tresses.
Marshes, bogs, meadows, and sandy beaches are habitats for
this plant, as are dry to moist woods, roadside ditches, and
grassy banks. The range is from Massachusetts to Florida west
to Texas and Nebraska.

3

Grass-leaved Ladies' Tresses

Spiránthes praècox

This small orchid flowers early and is quite variable in its makeup. Height varies from less than eight inches (2dm) to more than a foot (3dm). Five to seven very narrow leaves grow from the base of the stem but may not be present at flowering time. The plant is most variable in the positioning of its flowers. Usually there is a row in spiral arrangement, but it may be very loose or very tight, and sometimes all flowers may be on one side of the stalk. Each flower is one quarter inch to one half inch (6.2–12.5mm) long with a lip marked with radiating green lines. Flowering takes place from March to July. *S. vernalis*, Spring Ladies' Tresses, is similar, but the flowers are often tinged with yellow and without green markings. Grass-leaved Ladies' Tresses is also called Water Tresses and Giant Ladies' Tresses. Its habitats are marshes, bogs, meadows, low open woods, and roadside banks. It ranges from Rhode Island to Florida and west to Texas and Arkansas.

Pale Grass Pink

Calopògon pállidus

In most instances the flowers display a pale pink color and quite often are white with some of their parts curving forward and others backward. The stems are slender with very narrow grasslike foliage only at the base. Plant height varies from a foot to about two feet (3–6dm). Flowers averaging about an inch (2.5cm) in diameter appear from May to July. Their color varies from white or pink-tinged white to a very light pink. The oval sepals are curved back toward the stem. The lip is on the upper side of the flower and bears a tiny cluster of yellow hairs and often a pinkish purple mark. A wing-tipped column curves down and forward from the center of the flower. *C. pulchellus,* Grass Pink, has larger reddish pink flowers, and *C. barbatus,* Bearded Grass Pink, has a cluster of light pink flowers, all of them usually fully open while those of Pale Grass Pink are rarely all open at once. The habitats of Pale Grass Pink are open pine stands, meadows, savannahs, marshes, and swamps. The range is from southeastern Virginia to Florida west to Louisiana.

Rosebud Orchid

Cleìstes divaricàta

Slenderness is the essential feature of this willowy and graceful little orchid. Its greenish purple stem is usually about one and a half feet (4.5dm) tall but may be more than two feet (6dm). About midway up the stem is a single narrow leaf. The period of flowering is from May to July. One flower develops at the summit of the stem. Pink to purple or white petals converge to form a tube about two inches (.5dm) long. The lower petal or lip is tinted greenish yellow within and marked with purple. From the base of the flower three widely diverging reddish brown to purple sepals radiate upward. Rosebud Orchid is called also Spreading Pogonia, Rose Orchid, and Lady's Ettercap. It is found in swamps, savannahs, woods, and meadows. The range extends from New Jersey to Florida west to eastern Texas and Kentucky.

Shining Ladies' Tresses

Spirànthes lùcida

This is an attractive little orchid that displays glossy green leaves and white flowers that show a bright yellow spot. The stem is three to ten inches (.75–2.5dm) tall, its base sheathed by three to five leaves that are narrowed at both ends and three to six inches (.75–1.5dm) long. The flowers are in three to four rows that usually form spirals along the stem. Each flower is about one quarter inch to one half inch (6.2–12.5mm) long with a lip that bears a conspicuous yellow upper surface. The flowering period extends from May to July. The species *S. ovalis*, Oval Ladies' Tresses, also has several spirals of white flowers, but they are less than one quarter inch (6.2mm) long and have totally white lips. Shining Ladies' Tresses also has the name Wide-leaved Ladies' Tresses. It grows in moist woods and meadows, along stream banks, and in marshes. It ranges from Maine to western Virginia and Tennessee west to Kansas, Illinois, and Wisconsin.

Snowy Orchid

Habenària nívea

This is an orchid of open unshaded areas where the extreme whiteness of the flower clusters is such that their reflection of strong sunlight sometimes seems to lend them a blueish cast. The plant stands one to three feet (3–9dm) tall on a slender blue-green stem that has a few narrow erect leaves three to ten inches (.75–2.5dm) long near the base. The small flowers are about one half inch (12.5mm) and form a cluster in the shape of a cylinder or cone. The slender lip is uppermost and strongly curved back. The spur extends sideways and is usually curved upward at its tip. The flowering period is from May to September. Snowy Orchid also has been named Frog Spear and Bog Torch. It is a resident of bogs, wet meadows, savannahs, and open pine woods. It is present in southern New Jersey and Delaware and from eastern North Carolina to Florida west to Texas and Arkansas.

Round-leaved Orchid

Habenària orbiculàta

The foliage of this handsome orchid is as much a distinctive and ornamental feature as its floral display. The stout stem rises to a height of one to two feet (3–9dm) from between a pair of broad, rounded, and lustrous leaves that may be ten inches (2.5dm) long and very close to the same width. They rest flat upon the ground and are somewhat silvery on the underside. There are commonly ten to twenty white flowers that form a cylindrical cluster. The flower is oftentimes tinged with green and has a straight slender lip with a spur one to two inches (2.5–5cm) long that curves downward from its base. The flowering period is June to September. Large Round-leaved Orchid and Round-leaved Rein Orchid are also names for this species. Its habitats are dry to moist woods and infrequently bogs and swamps. The range is from Maine to the mountains of North Carolina, Tennessee, and Georgia, from West Virginia northwestward to Minnesota, and from Montana west to Washington and Oregon.

Downy Rattlesnake Plantain

Goodyèra pubéscens

Many diverse woodlands are hosts to this common orchid that is frequently found in dense and fairly extensive colonies and is remembered for its attractive foliage. The finely hairy stem is six inches to nearly two feet (1.5–6dm) tall with a circle of oval leaves one to three and a half inches (2.5–7.5cm) long at the base. The leaves are blueish green with a wide white or silvery mark down the middle and a similarly colored network of narrower marks over the remainder of the surface. The flower cluster has the shape of a cylinder or slender cone one to five inches (2.5–12.5cm) long. The tiny white flowers are almost round and only about one quarter inch (6.2mm) across. The flowering period runs from June to September. A second name for this species is Greater Lattice Leaf. It is at home in moist or dry wooded sites, and its foliage is present intact throughout the year. The plant has a range from Maine to Georgia west to Arkansas and Minnesota.

Lesser Rattlesnake Plantain

Goodyèra rèpens var. *ophioìdes*

The variegated leaves of this small orchid add patches of color to the shady floors of mountain forests. The plant is three inches to slightly over a foot (.75–3dm) tall. The hairy stem has a cluster of oval leaves a half inch to two inches (1.25–5cm) long at its base. They are usually dark blueish green with a variable pattern of white or silvery marking over the leaf surface. The midline of the leaf may be unmarked or weakly marked. The flower cluster is one to three and a half inches (2.5–8.8cm) long and usually one-sided. Flowers are less than one quarter inch (6.2mm) across. Flowering occurs from June to September. The northern Checkered Rattlesnake Plantain, *G. tesselata* extends southward only as far as Maryland and is very similar to Lesser Rattlesnake Plantain. It is generally a little larger plant in all parts. Lesser Rattlesnake Plantain is also called Lesser Lattice Leaf, Dwarf Rattlesnake Plantain, and Tessellated Lesser Rattlesnake Plantain. Habitats are cool moist woods, often on or near moss. The range is Maine to the mountains of North Carolina and Tennessee, from New York west to South Dakota, and from Idaho and Montana southeastward to New Mexico and Arizona.

Little Ladies' Tresses

Spiránthes gràyi

A neat spiral or a straight row of tiny white flowers on a wisp of a stem, Little Ladies' Tresses oftentimes makes its slimness more pronounced by attaining a height of two feet (6dm). Two or three small oval leaves are present on the base of the stem but usually wither before flowering occurs. The flower cluster is in the form of a tight or loose spiral, or sometimes it is a vertical line on one side of the stem. Each flower is entirely white and measures not more than one fifth of an inch (5mm) in length. These are the smallest flowers in this genus in the eastern United States. The flowering period is from June to September. Little Ladies' Tresses also bears the name Little Pearl Twist. The range extends from Massachusetts to Florida west to Texas and Missouri.

White Fringed Orchid

Habenària blephariglóttis

The large cluster of snow-white flowers at the top of a stem that is often almost four feet (1.2m) tall marks this as one of the most visible orchids. The stem is stout, and there are from two to four long, slender, and shiny leaves on the lower portion. The flower cluster is two to six inches (5–15cm) long and one to three inches (2.5–7.5cm) in diameter. The lip of the flower is about one half inch to nearly two inches (1.25–5cm) long, its border finely divided into a dense hair-like fringe. From the base of the lip a tubular spur curves backward and downward one to two inches (2.5–5cm). The flowering period is July to September. In the northern states the species tends to have flowers with shorter lips and spurs and to be smaller plants overall. From western North Carolina to Kentucky and south to Mississippi and Alabama there is a variety with a fringeless lip. White Fringed Orchid is also known as Plume-of-Navarre. It grows in the wet peaty soils of swamps, savannah ditches, bogs, and in pine barrens. The range is from Maine to Florida west to Texas and Michigan.

Three Birds

Triphora trianthóphora

Three Birds presents a different appearance from that of our other orchids by the presence of the small oval to heart-shaped leaves along the length of the stem. These leaves are about one half inch (12.5mm) long and green with a light or heavy tinting of purple. The green stem is also tinged with purple and stands three inches to one foot (.75–3dm) tall. From one to seven flowers may be produced, but it is common, however, for three flowers to develop at the sites of the three uppermost leaves. Flowers are white and very often flushed with pink or purple. The lip is about three quarters of an inch (18.5mm) long, its tip three-lobed and its upper surface marked by three green lines. The flowering period is from July to September. Nodding Pogonia, another name for the plant, lives in rich damp woods and thickets. It has a range from Maine to Florida west to Texas and Wisconsin.

Slender Ladies' Tresses

Spiránthes grácilis

A precise spiral of small white and densely crowded flowers is the trademark of this little orchid. The stem is slender and usually not more than one foot (3dm) tall. There are generally three to five oval leaves at ground level that may be withered by the time the flowers open from July to October. Flowers are one quarter inch (6.2mm) or less in length and white except for a green stripe on the upper surface of the lip. The names Southern Slender Ladies' Tresses and Long Tresses are also used for Slender Ladies' Tresses. It is a plant of dry sandy or rocky open woods, grassy fields and meadows, thickets, pastures, and roadsides. From Maine it ranges to Florida west to Texas, Kansas, and Michigan.

27

Nodding Ladies' Tresses

Spiránthes cérnua

Attractive colonies of this plant are sometimes seen brightening roadside ditches with their multiple spiraled white flower clusters. The stem is ordinarily six inches to two feet (1.5–6dm) tall but occasionally grows much taller. Three or four narrow leaves as much as one foot (3dm) long ascend from the base of the stem. During July to November the flowers appear in two to four dense rows. They are generally aligned in loose or tight spirals or straight lines; however at times the flower position seems to be random. The flowers are often fragrant, one quarter to one half inch (6.2–12.5mm) long, and slightly curved downward. Other names are Common Ladies' Tresses, Fragrant Ladies' Tresses, and Screw Auger. It is found often in small colonies growing in bogs, swamps, wet meadows, stream banks, moist open woods and fields, and along roadside ditches. Its range is from Maine to Florida west to Texas and North Dakota.

Long-bracted Orchid

Habenària víridis var. *bracteàta*

The long, slender, and pointed bracts or small leaves that protrude from the flower cluster earmark this orchid. The plant is about one to two feet (3–6dm) tall bearing two to five leaves, the lowermost of which are oval and often over six inches (15cm) long and nearly three inches (7.5cm) wide. The inconspicuous green flowers have a lip almost a half inch (12.5mm) long with two or three small teeth at the tip. A very small whitish saclike spur bulges from the underside of the lip. Beneath each flower there is a bract nearly an inch to two and one half inches (2.5–6.3cm) long. This species flowers from April to June. Other names are Long-bracted Green Orchid, Bracted Orchid, American Frog Orchid, and Satyr Orchid. It ranges from Maine to western North Carolina, from West Virginia west to South Dakota and Minnesota, from Montana south to New Mexico, and in Utah, Washington, and Alaska.

Large Whorled Pogonia

Isótria verticillàta

The breadth of the flower of this intriguing orchid may measure more than one fourth the height of the plant. The brownish or purplish stem is four inches to a little over a foot (1–3dm) tall. Near the summit there is a circle of five leaves about two to four inches (5–10cm) long. The three widely spreading sepals of the flower are greenish brown or purple and as much as two and one half inches (6.3cm) long. The yellowish green lateral petals meet to form a hood over the lip. The three-lobed lip has upturned outer lobes marked with purple and an expanded middle lobe that is white and often tinged with green or yellow. The flowering period is April to July. Each plant usually produces a single flower. Large Whorled Pogonia, also called Whorled Pogonia and Five-leaves, is similar in foliage to the common *Medeola virginiana,* but the former has hollow stems and the latter solid. The orchid grows in acid soils of moist or dry woods and along stream margins. Its range is from Maine to Florida west to Texas and Michigan.

Small Whorled Pogonia

Isótria medeoloìdes

Frequently cited as the rarest orchid in the eastern United States north of Florida, this small species is similar to Large Whorled Pogonia except for being essentially green throughout and having sepals an inch and a quarter (3cm) or less in length. There is a circle of five leaves at the top of a stem four to ten inches (1–2.5dm) tall that is green with an occasional tinge of purple. There is usually one green or pale yellowish green flower with spreading sepals and a lip that is often nearly white. The period of flowering is in May and June. Little Five-fingers, another name for this species, is a very rare resident of woodlands that is in need of protection from further disturbance. Its range extends, with a very few locations, from Maine to North Carolina with stations in Missouri and Michigan.

Yellow Twayblade

Líparis loesélii

A compact little orchid of pale and delicate beauty, its colors blend with its surroundings, making the plant easy to overlook. Its height varies from three inches to about a foot (.75–3dm). At the base of the stem there are two glossy light green leaves as much as eight inches long (2dm). A loose cluster of yellowish green to pale yellow flowers opens from May to July. The cluster is one to four inches (.25–1dm), each flower being about a half inch (12.5mm) in diameter with narrow to hairlike sepals and petals. The oblong lip is curved sharply downward and is grooved down the middle. The column is erect above the lip. Other names are Fen Orchid, Bog Twayblade, Russet Witch, Olive Scutcheon, and Loesel's Twayblade. It grows in wet woods, moist slopes and thickets, swamps, and bogs. The range extends from Maine southward to the mountains of North Carolina, from West Virginia northwestward to North Dakota, and in Alabama, Missouri, and Kansas.

Appalachian Twayblade

Listera smállii

Often beneath the spread of rhododendrons the cool moist slopes of the Appalachian Mountains harbor colonies of this slight orchid. The very slender green to brown stem is two inches to about a foot (.5–3dm) tall with a pair of kidney-shaped to nearly round leaves approximately midway. The tiny flowers are about a half inch (12.5mm) or less in length and usually brownish green to dark brown but may vary to shades of yellow, white, or pink. The lip is one quarter to a half inch (6.2–12.5mm) long with a pair of small rounded lobes at the base and a broad middle lobe cleft into two rounded or squarish lobes having a minute tooth between them. The flowers bloom in June and July. Appalachian Twayblade, known also as Kidney-leaved Twayblade and Small's Twayblade, is found in damp mountain woods, thickets, and bogs. It ranges from Pennsylvania down the Appalachian Mountains to Georgia.

Green Adder's Mouth

Maláxis unifòlia

An entirely green plant, this orchid has minute flowers and only a single leaf that clasps the stem at about its midpoint. The plant may be more than a foot and a half (4.5dm) tall. The leaf is oval and as much as three and a half inches (8.75cm) long with a base that wraps around the stem. The flowers are an eighth of an inch (3mm) or less in diameter. The lip is oblong and toothed at its tip. June to August is the flowering period. Species of the genus *Listera* are generally similar but do not have clasping leaves. Green Adder's Mouth lives in moist woods and thickets, meadows, and bogs. It has a range from Maine to Florida west to Texas and Minnesota.

Broad-leaved Helleborine

Epipáctis helleborine

This is a tall leafy orchid with a lengthy cluster of small flowers that frequently is greater than one third of the plant's height. There are three to ten oval to oblong leaves up to six inches (1.5dm) long and three inches (.75dm) wide on a stem that stands three to four feet (.9–1.2m) tall. The slender flower clusters may be four inches to one foot (1–3dm) long with narrow bracts or small leaves jutting from beneath the flowers. Each flower is about one half inch (12.5mm) across and commonly green with purple markings; there are, however, several combinations of green, purple, yellow, and pink displayed. The lip has the form of a tiny pouch with a triangular or heart-shaped tip that usually curves underneath the pouch. The time of flowering is from June to September. Helleborine tolerates many types of soil in woods, thickets, and roadsides. From New Hampshire it ranges to Virginia west to Missouri and Wisconsin and is also in Montana.

Green-fly Orchid

Epidéndrum conópseum

Searching for this evergreen orchid almost always involves a considerable amount of time spent looking up. It is an epiphytic species that grows upon other plants but does not parasitize them. The stem is slender and two inches to about a foot (.5–3dm) tall with seldom more than three leaves. They are glossy dark green and leathery with narrow blades pointed at both ends. The flowers develop from July to September in elongated and sometimes branched clusters. The small flowers are rarely much more than an inch (2.5cm) across and vary from yellowish green to grayish green that is sometimes tinted with purple. The lip has three rounded or angular lobes. The flowers are fragrant. Green-fly Orchid grows, often in tufts, upon several species of trees in woods and swamps and sometimes on rocks. From extreme southeastern North Carolina it ranges along the coastal plain to Florida and along the Gulf Coast to Louisiana.

Florida Adder's Mouth

Maláxis spicàta

Otherwise totally green, the maturing flowers are touched with tiny spots of orange. The plant's height may be a foot and a half (4.5dm) but is more often eight inches (2dm) or less. There are two bright green leaves whose bases clasp the stem near its base or near the midpoint. The flowers are very small and green but with age take on tints of yellow or brown. The lip is uppermost about an eighth of an inch (3mm) long and reddish orange at maturity. Its shape is oval with a pointed or blunt tip directed upward. Flowers are open from July to September. Members of the genus *Listera* are somewhat similar, but their leaves do not clasp the stem. Florida Adder's Mouth is also called Florida Malaxis and Little Orange Lip. It ranges from southeastern Virginia along the coastal plain to Florida.

Shadow Witch

Ponthièva racemòsa

The green rosettes, reddish stems, and pale flowers of this coastal orchid compose attractive colonies that spread through wet, shady habitats. The greenish red to reddish brown or purple stem may attain a height of two feet (6dm). The bright green leaves in a circle at the base of the stem are as much as seven inches (1.75dm) long. The flowers open from September to October and are one quarter inch to one half inch (6.2-12.5mm) across. They are whitish with strong green veining. The pouchlike lip is uppermost and has a pointed tip. Lateral sepals form a shieldlike or diamond shape below, hiding the lowest sepal underneath. The lateral sepals are on either side of the lip. Other names are Ponthieu's Orchid and Glandular Neottia. It grows in the calcium soils of damp woods, woodland stream banks, and pond borders. The range is from southeastern Virginia along the coastal plain to Florida west to Texas.

Southern Rein Orchid

Habenària flàva var. *herbiòla*

This is a leafy, deep green orchid of wet places that exhibits more leafiness and a stouter stem in the mountains and to the north. Its height varies from less than a foot to nearly three feet (3–9dm). There are two to five leaves up to eight inches (2dm) long and two inches (.5dm) wide. The small flowers are yellow-green with a lip about one quarter inch (6.2mm) long curved beneath the flower. The base of the lip has a tooth or tiny lobe on each side and another tooth, the tubercle, about in the center of the upper surface. Beneath each flower is a bract or small leaf the lower ones often over an inch (2.5cm) long. Plants of western Virginia, the Carolinas, and western Kentucky and Tennessee have bracts the length of the flowers or shorter. Flowering is from March to September. Other names are Tubercled Orchid and Pale Green Orchid. It grows in flood plains, bogs, marshes, and wet meadows and woods. The range is from Maine to Florida west to Texas and Minnesota.

Yellow Lady's Slipper

Cypripèdium calcèolus

One of the most familiar of our orchids, this species displays a flower noteworthy for its brightness and size and for its unusual shape. It may stand almost three feet (9dm) tall, the stout hairy stem usually bearing three to six oval leaves one to five inches (2.5–12.5cm) wide. One or two flowers develop from April to June. The "slipper" is less than an inch to slightly over two and one half inches (2.5–6.3cm) long. Plants of swamps and bogs with small flowers are often cited as a variety. A species of northern Kentucky, *C. candidum* or Small White Lady's Slipper, is similar to the smaller plants, but its "slipper" is white. Handling of leaves and stems of Yellow Lady's Slipper, also called Yellow Moccasin Flower, Golden Slipper, and Whip-poor-will Shoe, is said to cause skin inflammation in some people. The plant lives in moist woods, along wet shores, and in bogs and swamps. It ranges from Maine to Georgia west to Texas and North Dakota and from New Mexico northwestward to Washington.

Water Spider Orchid

Habenària rèpens

The name is indicative of both the habitat and appearance of this orchid because wading is usually required for a close look at its flowers, which do indeed resemble spiders. Nearly the entire length of the slender one to three foot (3–9dm) stem bears narrow pointed leaves two to ten inches (.5–2.5dm) long. The flowers that appear from April to November are pale greenish yellow and about one half inch (12.5mm) in diameter. The lip is cleft nearly to its base into very slender lobes, the outer lobes almost hairlike. A spur about one half inch (12.5mm) long curves backward and downward from the flower. The lateral petals are also cleft into two thin lobes that curve upward. Another species, *H. quinqueseta* or Michaux's Orchid, is similar but distinguishable by its larger flowers with a white lip and a spur one and a half to seven inches (3.75–17.5cm) long. Water Spider Orchid is found in lakes, streams, swamps, wet ditches, and pools. Its range extends from eastern North Carolina along the coastal plain to Florida west along the gulf coast to Texas.

Pale Coral Root

Corallorhiza trifida

This small orchid growing in damp woods forms small colonies whose pale color contrasts sharply with the shade. The stems of the plant are yellow or greenish yellow and not more than a foot (3dm) tall. Flowers of May to July are about one half inch (12.5mm) in diameter and yellow except for the lip. The white lip is less than a quarter inch (6.2mm) long with two tiny lateral lobes and a rounded or notched middle lobe. Beneath the lip's base is a small swelling. Plants in the north tend to grow in drier woods and have purple spots on the lip as well as other flower parts. *C. wisteriana*, or Spring Coral Root, may be yellow but normally has purple coloring in most parts and an unlobed lip with no swelling beneath. Pale Coral Root, also called Early Coral Root and Northern Coral Root, is found in damp woods, swamps, and thickets and ranges from Maine to Virginia west to Missouri and Minnesota and from Washington, Idaho, and Montana southeastward to New Mexico.

Little Club-spur Orchid

Habenària clavellàta

A small plant with very small flowers, this diminutive orchid has sparse foliage, usually consisting of a single leaf and is only four inches (1dm) to about one foot (3dm) tall. On the ridged stem there is generally one oblong leaf four to seven inches (1–1.75dm) long and occasionally a second such leaf. The flowers are pale yellow or greenish yellow and about one quarter inch (6.2mm) in diameter. The lip is almost rectangular with three rounded teeth at the tip and a slender spur about one half inch (12.5mm) long that curves downward beneath or beside the flower. The tip of the spur is somewhat enlarged. Flowering occurs from June to September. Other names are Green Woodland Orchid, Small Green Wood Orchid, Small Green Orchid, Wood Orchid, and Frog Spike. It grows in moist woods and meadows, bogs, swamps, and thickets. The range is from Maine to Florida west to Texas and Minnesota.

Ragged Fringed Orchid

Habenària lácera

The clusters of finely dissected flowers give a tattered look
that is the conspicuous feature of this species. The plant's
height varies from one foot to about two and one half feet
(3–7.5dm). The stem is sheathed with four to nine narrow
pointed leaves, some leaves over eight inches (2dm) long. The
flowers that appear from June to September are pale yellow to
greenish yellow. The lip is deeply cleft into three lobes, each
of which is in turn divided irregularly into narrow to hairlike
portions. A slender spur one half to one inch (1.25–2.5cm)
long curves downward underneath the lip. *H. repens,* Water
Spider Orchid, is similar in general form and in color, but the
three lobes of its lip are not further divided. Ragged Fringed
Orchid is known also as Green Fringed Orchid and Ragged
Orchid. It frequents wet woods, roadside ditches, wet meadows, swamps, marshes, and bogs. From Maine it ranges south
to Georgia west to Texas and Minnesota.

Crested Fringed Orchid

Habenària cristàta

Compact cylindrical to oval clusters of golden yellow or saffron flowers mark the position of this plant among the grasses of meadows and savannahs. The sturdy stem stands eight inches to three feet (2–9dm) tall with a few narrow pointed leaves as much as eight inches (2dm) long at the base. The flowering season is from June to September. The flowers are about a third of an inch (8.3mm) in diameter and vary in color from orange to orange-yellow or pale yellow. The fringed lip is about a quarter of an inch (6.2mm) long with a spur about the same length extending back from its base. *H. ciliaris*, Yellow Fringed Orchid, is a similar species with flowers one half inch (12.5mm) or more across and a much longer spur. Crested Fringed Orchid is also known as Yellow Fringed Orchid, Orange Crest Orchid, and Crested Yellow Orchid. It is found in bogs, swamps, meadows, and savannahs. The range is from Massachusetts to Florida west to Texas and Arkansas.

Yellow Fringeless Orchid

Habenària intégra

This trim and colorful little orchid hugs the coastal and southern boundaries of the Middle Atlantic states. The stem is one to two feet (3–6dm) tall and bears only very small leaves for most of its length, but one or two narrow leaves four to ten inches (1–2.5dm) long sprout from near the base. The flowers open from July to September forming dense clusters in the shape of a cone or cylinder. The color may be orange or yellow. The lip is about one quarter inch (6.2mm) long or less and oval or oblong with a rounded or pointed tip. Its borders are usually wavy or irregularly toothed. A spur approximately one quarter inch (6.2mm) long extends behind the flower. Southern Yellow Orchid, Yellow Orchid, and Golden Frog Arrow are other names for this species. It frequents swamps, open bogs, wet meadows, savannahs, and pine barrens. From New Jersey the range extends south to Florida and west to Texas and Tennessee.

Yellow Fringed Orchid

Habenària ciliáris

This is one of the most strikingly handsome of the native orchids with its flower clusters that resemble bright orange flares. The stem is a foot to over three feet (3–9dm) tall and bears several narrow pointed leaves, some of which are about a foot (3dm) long. Flowers open from July to September forming clusters two or three inches (5–7.5cm) thick and up to six inches (1.5dm) long. The flowers are about one half inch (12.5mm) in diameter and vary from deep orange to yellowish orange. The finely fringed lip is about one half inch (12.5mm) long with a slender spur an inch to an inch and a half (2.5–3.75cm) curving downward from its base. *H. cristata,* Crested Fringed Orchid, is a similar species but has smaller flowers with a much shorter spur. Yellow Fringed Orchid is also called Orange Plume. It is found in swamps, bogs, meadows, thickets, and sandy woods. From Massachusetts its range extends to Florida and west to Texas and Michigan.

Bicolored Fringed Orchid

Habenària x *bicolor*

This plant has long been considered a hybrid, as indicated by the x entered in the scientific name, of the White Fringed Orchid, *H. blephariglottis,* and the Yellow Fringed Orchid, *H. ciliaris.* The species believed to be the parents have the same habitats, and their flowering periods overlap. The general structure of the supposed hybrid is the same as that of the assumed parents, and the color of the flowers is intermediate between yellowish orange and white. The flowers are usually pale yellowish orange or cream, and often the fringed lip or upper parts that form the hood are white. The range is from Maine to Florida west to Texas and Michigan.

Bearded Grass Pink

Calopògon barbàtus

Less common than the other grass pinks, the floral cluster at the top of this spindly plant usually has all its flowers fully open at the same time. The very slender stem is green to reddish brown and half a foot to one and a half feet (1.5–4.5dm) tall. There are one or two leaves at the base about six inches (1.5dm) long and grasslike. In April and May the light pink (or rarely white) flowers open. They are about an inch (2.5cm) across with a lip on the upper side about one half inch (12.5mm) long and crested with a small patch of yellow hairs. The curved and winged column projects from the center of the flower. Generally there are three to six flowers. *C. pulchellus*, Grass Pink, and *C. pallidus*, Pale Grass Pink, have flowers that open successively up the stem, those of the former being larger and deep to reddish pink, while the latter's are white to pale pink with sepals curved back. Bearded Grass Pink grows in pinelands, meadows, and savannahs. Its range is from North Carolina to Florida west to Louisiana along the coast.

Showy Orchid

Órchis spectábilis

There are usually two to ten bicolored flowers borne
upon a leafy stalk that rises from between two broad leaves
at ground level and attains a height of two or three inches
(5–7.5cm) to more than a foot (3dm). The leaves are glossy
and somewhat sticky and measure three to eight inches (.75–
2dm) in length. Commonly the lip of the flower is white and
has a tubular spur that extends downward about the length of
the lip. The sepals and lateral petals converge to form a pink
to purple hood that overhangs the lip. Color varies so that
the lip may be partially or completely pink or purple, and occasionally the entire flower is white. The flowering period is
from April to July. Showy Orchid is also called Purple-hooded
Orchid and Two-leaved Orchid. Its habitats are rich open hard-
wood forests, moist slopes, and stream banks. The range extends
from Maine to Georgia west to Arkansas and Minnesota.

Pink Lady's Slipper

Cypripèdium acaùle

A relatively common orchid, Pink Lady's Slipper is found more often in drier places than are the other lady's slippers. The leafless stem can be nearly two feet (6dm) tall arising from between a pair of broad oval leaves at its base. There is a single flower with a "slipper" about two inches (5cm) long that is cleft down the middle and is usually reddish pink with purple veining or infrequently all white. The flower parts above the slipper are shades of green, yellow, brown, and purple. The period of flowering is from April to July. Other names are Pink Moccasin Flower, Moccasin Flower, Nerve Root, and Stemless, Common, or Two-leaved Lady's Slipper. Its habitats are dry woodlands, bogs, and swamps. The range extends from Maine to Georgia and Alabama and from Ohio north-westward to Minnesota.

Dragon's Mouth

Arethùsa bulbòsa

This open-mouthed dragon with the erect ears may rear its head only a few inches (2.5cm) to more than a foot (3dm) from the ground. There are no leaves present when the usually lone flower opens. It is one inch to two and a half inches (2.5–6.25cm) long and most often purplish pink but may be lilac or occasionally white. The lip is curved downward and is pale to deep pink with variable purple markings and a "beard" of three or more lines of white to yellow hairs. Flowering occurs in May and June. *Pogonia ophioglossoides,* Rose Pogonia, is somewhat similar but has an oval leaf one to seven inches (.25–1.75dm) long at about the middle of its stem as well as another smaller leaf just below the flower, and its lip has a deeply fringed margin. Dragon's Mouth, also called Bog Rose, Swamp Pink, and Wild Pink, is a very rare orchid of bogs, meadows, swamps, and woods from Maine to New Jersey west to Illinois and Minnesota, and in just a very few locations in Virginia and North Carolina.

Rose Pogonia

Pogònia ophioglossoìdes

This graceful plant has a slender stem bearing a solitary leaf at about its middle and a bright pink flower at its summit. Height of the green to brownish or purplish stem varies from a very few inches (2.5cm) to a little over two feet (6dm). The rather narrow leaf is two to six inches (.5-1.5dm) long. Flowering occurs from May to August, sometimes producing two or three flowers. The flower parts are about one inch (2.5cm) long and generally pink or infrequently white. The lip is oblong to spoon-shaped with a "beard" of yellow hairs and a fringed purple lip. *Arethusa bulbosa,* Dragon's Mouth, is somewhat similar but has no leaves or fringed lip margin. Rose Pogonia is also known as Pogonia, Beard Flower, and Snake Mouth. Its habitats are open bogs and meadows, savannahs, and seepage slopes. Its range is from Maine to Florida west to Texas, in Missouri, and from eastern Kentucky northwestward to Minnesota.

Grass Pink

Calopògon pulchéllus

The showy flowers provide spots of bright pink color in the flat, open, and grassy terrain in which it grows. The stem is four inches to over four feet (.1–1.2m) tall with a few long narrow leaves at the base. During the period from May to August the flowers open with a color range from pale to purplish pink and occasionally white. The lip is on the upper side and is one half inch to nearly an inch (1.25–2.5cm) long with an enlarged squarish tip and a tuft of yellow hairs. At the center of the flower is the down-curved column. Flowers are about an inch and a half (3.75cm) in diameter and open in succession up the stem. *C. pallidus,* or Pale Grass Pink, and *C. barbatus,* Bearded Grass Pink, have smaller flowers, and those of the former are usually very pale to white, while those of the latter all open at about the same time. Grass Pink also has been named Swamp Pink and Rose Wings. It is a plant of open bogs, meadows, swamps, and savannahs. It ranges from Maine to Florida west to Texas and Minnesota.

Queen Lady's Slipper

Cypripèdium regìnae

This stately orchid is extremely rare in the Middle Atlantic region. Its stout hairy stem is a foot to more than three feet (3–9dm) tall with three to eight broad sheathing leaves four to ten inches (1–2.5dm) long. There are usually one or two flowers and sometimes three or four. The "slipper" is about two inches (5cm) long and generally reddish pink with furrowed streaks of white but may vary to all purple or all white. The parts above the slipper are oval to nearly round and intensely white. Flowering takes place from May to early September. Other names are Showy Lady's Slipper, Large White Lady's Slipper, and Big Pink and White. The hairs of the stems and leaves reportedly cause mild to severe skin irritation. Unfortunately this has not been sufficient to deter those who would remove this species from the wild. It grows in bogs, swamps, and wet woods. The range is from Maine south westward to northern Alabama west to Missouri and North Dakota.

Spring Coral Root

Corallorhìza wisteriàna

The earliest flowering of our coral roots, the entire plant is usually strongly tinged with purplish or reddish brown with only the flowers showing spots of white. The greenish to purplish brown stem is four inches to nearly a foot and a half (1–4.5dm) tall with tubular sheaths around the lower portion. The sepals and lateral petals are about one third of an inch (8.3mm) long and are purplish or reddish brown or greenish yellow with purple or brown mottling. They form a hood over the strongly down-curved lip which is white with purple dots and has a rounded and notched tip. The flowers open from late March until May. Early Southern Coral Root and Wister's Coral Root are other names for this species. This is a plant that carries on no photosynthesis. It is found in moist woods, rich ravines, swamps, and along stream margins. The range is from New Jersey to Florida west to Texas and Kansas, in South Dakota, and from Montana south to New Mexico and Arizona.

Southern Twayblade

Lístera austràlis

But for its pair of small green leaves this plant is usually darkly purple or purplish green, making it difficult to locate in the deep shade of the sites it inhabits. Two ovate leaves grow opposite one another about midway of a slender stem that is one half to a foot (1.5–3dm) tall. The flowers open from April to July and are reddish purple to greenish purple. The lip is about one half inch (12.5mm) long and divided at its tip into two prongs with a minute tooth between them. Another species, *L. cordata* or Heartleaf Twayblade, very rare in the mid-Atlantic region, also has a two-pronged lip, but it is only half as long and has a pair of distinct hornlike teeth at its base. Southern Twayblade is a plant of low moist woods, pine barrens, thickets, and bogs. It is in Vermont, New York, New Jersey, and Tennessee, and from Virginia to Florida west to Texas.

Putty Root

Apléctrum hyemàle

About a dozen purplish flowers are clustered loosely at the top of a leafless stem that is enclosed below by tubular sheaths and is one to two feet (3–6dm) tall. The flowers measure about one inch (2.5cm) across and are frequently greenish purple tinged with yellow but may vary to purple, brown, or whitish. The lip is usually white with a wavy margin and a smaller lobe on either side. The flowering period is May and June. Putty Root is known as well by the name Adam-and-Eve. Both names come from a pair of rounded corms or underground stems that have a slender connection between them. The corms contain a sticky substance that has been used in mending pottery. This plant lives in rich woods, alluvial plains, and swamps. It has a range from Vermont to Georgia west to Arkansas and Minnesota.

Large Twayblade

Liparis lilifòlia

No more than a foot (3dm) tall, this dainty orchid is similar in general form to Yellow Twayblade, *L. loeselii*, but has larger flowers which are purplish. The stem is two to ten inches (.5–2.5dm) tall with a pair of bright green leaves two to seven inches (.5–1.75dm) long clasping the base. The flowers open from May to July forming a cluster about two to six inches (.5–1.5dm) long. Each flower is approximately one inch (2.5cm) in diameter with pale green narrow sepals, two of which are behind the lip. The threadlike lateral petals are purple and curved downward. The rounded lip is about a half inch (12.5mm) long and pale purple to brownish purple with one or more tiny pointed tips at the apex. The column protrudes above the lip. Other names are Mauve Sleekwort, Purple Scutheon, and Lily-leaved Twayblade. Moist wooded slopes, floodplains, and stream banks are its habitats. The range is New Hampshire to Georgia west to Missouri and Minnesota.

Purple Fringed Orchid

Habenària psychòdes

The form and size of the colorful flowers and flower clusters rank the Purple Fringed Orchid as one of the most impressive of our native orchids. The stem is eight inches to five feet (.2–1.5m) tall bearing two to five oval leaves as much as nine inches (2.25dm) long. Flowers open from June to August producing clusters as long as eight inches (2dm) and as thick as two inches (.5dm). Each lilac to magenta or sometimes white flower is about half an inch to over an inch (1.25–2.5cm) in diameter. The lip is about a half inch to an inch (1.25–2.5cm) wide and deeply cleft into three flared and finely fringed lobes. From the base of the lip a slender tubular spur extends backward, its opening either dumbbell-shaped or round. Plants with the larger flowers and the rounded spur opening are cited as a variety or sometimes as a separate species. Purple Fringed Orchid, also called Butterfly Orchid and Soldier's Plume, is found in wet woods, meadows, pastures, and swamps. It ranges from Maine to the mountains of North Carolina and Tennessee, and Georgia west to Arkansas and Minnesota.

Spiked Medusa

Eulòphia ecristàta

This curiously attractive orchid attains heights that allow a close look at the odd arrangement of its angled flowers at standing eye level. The leafless stem ascends to a height of two to more than five feet (.61–1.5m). There is a cluster of narrow pleated and grasslike leaves which are often over two feet (6dm) long at the base of the stem. The flowers that come from June to September are about one half inch (12.5mm) long and are greenish yellow to bronze or brown with various purple markings. The lip is purple to brown and lies under the overhanging sepals and lateral petals. The flowers are bent at a right angle, and narrow pointed bracts or small leaves as much as two and a half inches (6.25cm) long extend from beneath them. The habitats of this orchid include moist woods, fields, pinelands, and dry grassy clearings. The plant is distributed along the coastal plain from eastern North Carolina to Florida west to southern Louisiana.

Purple Fringeless Orchid

Habenària peramoèna

A striking orchid sometimes displaying a dense cluster of rose-purple flowers seven inches (1.75dm) long and two inches (5cm) thick, Purple Fringeless Orchid does not grow too far outside the Middle Atlantic region. It stands a foot to three and a half feet (3–1.05m) tall and has two to four lower leaves that are four to eight inches (1–2dm) long with several much smaller ones above. The flowers bloom from June to October and are about three quarters of an inch (1.8cm) in diameter. The lip is deeply divided into three lobes, the tips of which have small teeth. The middle lobe is wider and notched. A slender spur with an enlarged tip curves downward about an inch (2.5cm) from the base of the lip. *H. psychodes* or Purple Fringed Orchid is a similar species but has the lateral petals finely toothed and the lip deeply fringed and not notched. Purple Fringeless Orchid, also called Pride-of-the-Peak, grows in wet meadows, woods, and thickets, and in roadside ditches. It ranges from southern New Jersey and western New York southwestward to Mississippi and Missouri.

Crested Coral Root

Hexaléctris spicàta

This flesh-colored orchid with the striped flowers is similar to but much more striking than the coral roots of the genus *Corallorhiza*. The stem, which may be slender or stout, reaches one to more than two and a half feet (3–7.5dm). The leaves are very small and scalelike, and both leaves and stem may be lightly or heavily tinted with purple. The flowering period is July and August. The flowers are yellow or whitish and streaked with reddish to brownish purple. They are about one inch (2.5cm) across with a yellow or white three-lobed lip that is normally darkly marked with reddish purple ridges. The column is white. Crested Coral Root, also called Cockscomb and Brunetta, does not carry on photosynthesis. Its habitats are dry to somewhat moist open deciduous forests and woodland stream banks. The range is from Maryland and West Virginia to Florida west to Arizona, Arkansas, and Missouri.

Cranefly Orchid

Tipulària discolor

A slim leafless stem bears a narrow column of small delicate flowers whose spreading threadlike parts suggest a swarm of purplish insects. The brownish to yellowish green stem is tinged with purple and usually eight inches to two feet (2–6dm) tall. The flowers are often purple but may show shades of green, yellow, or rust. They are about one half inch (12.5mm) in diameter and have a lip less than one half inch (12.5mm) long with a narrow central lobe and a rounded lobe on each side at the base. There is a slender tubular spur about an inch (2.5cm) long that extends backward from the base of the lip. The flowering period is from July to September. Cranefly Orchid is also known as Elfin Spur. It is usually found in rich damp woods. Its range extends from eastern New York and Massachusetts to Florida west to Texas and Michigan.

Spotted Coral Root

Corallorhìza maculàta

Extensive colonies are often formed by this orchid sending up a host of purple to bronze stems topped with elongate clusters of small flowers. The stems are one to two feet (3–6dm) tall, their leaves reduced to a few encircling sheaths. The flowers are one half inch to three quarters of an inch (1.25–1.8cm) in diameter and about the same color as the stem with the exception of the white lip. The lip is spotted purple and three-lobed with a small swelling underneath its base. The column shows as a yellow spot in the center of the flower. Flowering takes place from July to September. No photosynthetic activity is evident. Other names for this species are Large Coral Root and Many-flowered Coral Root. It grows in the rich humus of shady woods and stream banks. Its range is from Maine to the mountains of North Carolina, Tennessee, and Georgia west to Minnesota and Iowa, from Idaho and Montana southeast to western Nebraska, south to Texas and Arizona, and from Washington to California.

Autumn Coral Root

Corallorhiza odontorhiza

Having small flowers that characteristically remain unopened as well as a lack of bright colors make this species the least attractive of our coral root orchids. The very slender stem is four inches to a foot and a half (1–4.5dm) tall and yellowish to purplish brown. The period of flowering is from August to October. The sepals and lateral petals of the tiny flowers are about a fifth of an inch (5mm) long and pale green to yellow with purple tinting. They extend as a hood over the shorter lip which is white with purple specks. The lower flowers of the cluster are almost always enlarged in fruit development. This species is very similar to *C. wisteriana*, Spring Coral Root, but differs in its smaller and unopened flowers and larger amount of green coloring. Other names for Autumn Coral Root are Late Coral Root and Small Coral Root. It is a plant of dry woodlands and ranges from Maine to Florida west to Texas and southeastern Nebraska.

Index of Common and Scientific Names

The color group of each species is indicated.